Life's Instruction Book

FOR WOMEN

Volume II

Barbara Gray

Published by Barbara Gray Proactives
399 Old Canton Road, Marietta, Georgia 30068

ISBN 0-9637784-1-2

Printed by Vaughan Printing
Nashville, Tennessee

To

Anne, my best friend.
   Thank you for letting me check in each day.
Mary Charles
   You are going to do great!
Diane Benton
   Thanks for your insights.
Akbar
   You've taught me so much.

General Instructions for Daily Living
Instructions for Relationships
Steps for Success
Discovering Your Inner Self
Self Worth
Relating to Men
Success After Divorce

General Instructions for Living

1. You can hide your tears internally, in the shower, the rain, or not at all, but you feel the pain all the same.

2. Never put anything on paper you wouldn't read in front of a jury.

3. **Your best book of instruction is the Bible.**

4. It's not necessary to argue your point, but stand firm on it.

5. **STRESS**
   <u>S</u>igns
   <u>T</u>hat
   <u>R</u>equire
   <u>E</u>ase
   <u>S</u>implicity
   <u>S</u>elf

6. Find a church where you feel comfortable and one that meets your needs. In return, you should make the church comfortable and meet it's needs.

7. Your posture and your walk, more than anything, makes you look young or old.

8. Fight fair.

9. Don't wait until a tragedy teaches you what is important about life. You might never experience one to find out.

10. Unfortunately, you find out what your friends think of you when they fix you up with a blind date.

11. The best response to someone trying to mind your business is, "Why do you think you need to know?"

12. Refuse to give up on what you believe.

13. Rapid refunds from your taxes are the most costly mistake you can make.

14. Why use concealer for your blemishes,
    if you open your mouth and reveal
    your worst flaws?

15. Never get a car loan for over three years or house mortgages for over fifteen years. It will save you thousands of dollars.

16. It is not safe to have permanent make-up applied in a mall.

17. Start improving yourself by changing one thing at a time.

18. Keep at it when you're on a roll —
    sometimes momentum is everything.

19. When you preplan, you won't have to
    use ATM's, and it will be a lot safer.

20. Asking a person to "*Give me your word*," is the best guarantee for responsibility and honesty.

21. Support small self-owned independent stores.

22. ***Develop perspective thinking*** rather than myopic thinking – or focusing too direct or too long on one aspect.

23. Great ideas are not born in bars or in front of the television.

24. Live your life to the fullest, not the foolish.

25. **Sheep mentality gets you pregnant, broke, or broken-hearted.**

26. Keep your promises or have an honest explanation of why you didn't.

27. Think out the consequences of getting what you ask for.

28. Find good role models for your daughter.

29. Analyze the purpose of your shopping. Do you not have anything better to do?

30. Keep a sense of *spontaneity*. Give into it's impulses to seize the moment. Spontaneous moments spark life.

31. Call people by the names they call themselves. Don't change their names.

32. *Women take chances on the men in their lives rather than themselves.*

33. If you're not reading good books, you are starving your mind.

34. Protect your children from second hand smoke.

35. If we'll buy shampoo to liven hair that is already dead, then we're gullible to buy pills to lose weight while we sleep and cream to remove cellulite.

36. Travel, real or imagined, fulfills life and helps you choose the best place to live.

37. Lives, like scratched records, will play the same tune over and over if you don't take action.

38. Stop scams, con artists and hard-nosed salespeople who push you into bad decisions by shoving immediacy down your throat. If a decision does not feel right going down, it will turn sourer when it lands.

39. Change your name if you're stuck with one that you don't like or doesn't suit you anymore.

40. Avoid being a woman whose life consists of reading romance novels and pretends to be someone you're not.

41. **Most things are never so bad that there isn't a solution to the problem or the solution is accepting the problem.**

42. The best answer to "Can you do me a favor?" is "*Let me know what it is, so I can think about it.*"

43. Look at your problems as if you're flying in an airplane and they become smaller.

44. Teach your children by example.

45. It's never too late to get braces for crooked teeth.

46. You spend the first half of your life learning what to do with the second half.

47. Lies are passed down – if you love me, you will have sex with me, a wife is a man's property.

48. **Support the quality movies written and directed by women**. They are filled with emotion, truth, and beauty.

49. Hire an ugly babysitter.

50. People like to use the vocabulary pertaining to their occupations to intimidate you.

51. Tell your children about your past. It helps them understand your present.

52. Teach your daughter the consequences of an abortion.

53. Do what you have to do.

54. Teach your daughter never to sell herself short.

55. Children remember more what you didn't do for them than what you did.

56. *Ask the people who know so much about how to run your life, what they are doing in theirs.*

57. The news spends more time scaring us about the things that will kill us rather than emphasizing the things that make us live.

58. Foolish people follow people who say things just to be outrageous.

59. Takers lose the rewards of giving.

60. Keep your schedule open so that when you are in the mood to do really important things in life, you are able to jump on them.

61. People are like snakes – poisonous and non-poisonous. You can identify them by their markings, sometimes we choose to ignore markings.

62. We steal our own happiness when we
    don't make an effort to enjoy what
    makes us happy.

63. Don't use the words everyone else is using.

64. *Simple things like blowing bubbles and sparklers are still the most fun.*

65. You're more likely to fall off a ladder when someone at the bottom yells to be more careful.

66. Since you would fight for your life in the face of death, why not fight for your life while you can make such great changes.

67. Read to discover whether you are auditory, visual or kinesthetic; that will explain much of your behavior.

68. *Most arguments are like getting in a mud fight. You might win, but you had to get dirty to do it.*

69. Apply make-up to enhance.

70. People, who think life isn't fair, think that they have some promises on their birth certificate.

71. *We pretend our lives are movies directed by others while we follow a script that keeps our real self hidden.*

72. *Smart women spend their time talking about ideas rather than people.*

73. Read...not because you have nothing else to do. Set a time to treat yourself and then read.

74. Keep improving your posture.

75. **Ask people to pray for you.**

76. Keep an extra pair of pantyhose in your car.

77. Riding someone else's coat tail can mean a rough ride.

78. Learning to line dance is fun, free, and great exercise.

79. We are not glued to one spot on this earth. Find your best growing conditions. *Do what you have to do to thrive in your world.* A comfort zone awaits you.

80. Defend one who is absent – even at the bridge table.

81. Watch out for the *false sayings* that have become popular-
Life's a Bitch...vs. **Life is What You Choose**.
The One Who Has The Most Toys Wins...
vs. **The One Who Fulfills Her Needs Wins**.
You Can't Teach An Old Dog New Tricks...
vs. **Good Things Come To Those Who Are Willing To Change**.

82. Learn to barter.

83. Be a love finder rather than a fault finder.

84. Smart women spend their time talking about ideas rather than people.

85. *Watch Steel Magnolias once a year!*

86. Be your own best friend.

87. All the manufactures are claiming that their foods are low-fat or fat-free. The formula to figure out how much fat the product really has is : *Take the number of fat grams x 9 = X. X is divided by the total number of calories* – that will equal the amount of fat per serving. Also, check and see if it's a realistic serving.

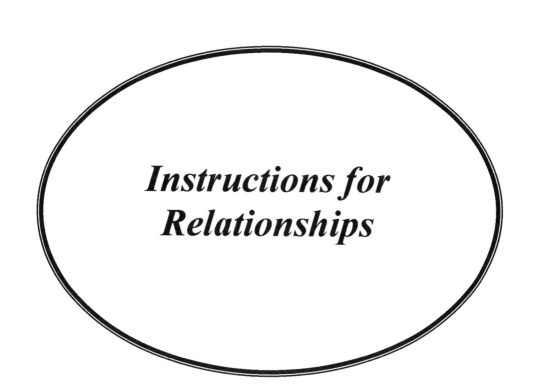

*Instructions for
Relationships*

1. **Write a letter to the person with whom you are having a problem.** One, they will read it, two, you are better able to express your thoughts, and lastly the writing will put the problem in better perspective.

2. ***Being in love shouldn't hurt.***

3. Expand your criteria for a potential mate.

4. You must be intimate with yourself before you can be intimate with others.

5. Mothers are travel agents for guilt trips.

6. We desire the feeling of connectedness with all humanity.

7. If you take another woman's husband, you lose the chance to find out what's wrong with him.

8. It is essential to have friends with whom you can be totally honest.

9. Start praying today for a good daughter-in-law or a good mother-in-law.

10. Your problem child is the one most like you.

11. The kind of CEO's women should be looking for are: ***Completers, Empowerers of Others.***

12. Know the person rather than assign them to generalities.

13. Total honesty may cost a lot of time, but the dividends are great for those who pay the price.

14. Look for a man more interested in giving you love than taking your love.

15. Flowers, gifts and jewelry are nice, but a man who gives you total acceptance gives you the gift of total love.

16. If you don't devote time to your mate while you're raising the kids, you won't know him when they're gone.

17. You can still wear your crown even if your children disappoint you. **The Queen of England does.**

18. Don't let others push you into quick decisions.

19. The things that are at the top of your agenda may not be at the top of his agenda, so you better be prepared to communicate the importance and position of your needs.

20. Children can break up second marriages, so **be prepared to work harder in a blended family**.

21. Searching for a mate for self-enhancement rather than love assures a failed relationship.

22. Lovers may disappoint and hurt us, but love never does, so don't give up on love.

23. Seek trust and intimacy in sex rather than performance.

24. **We seek our own level of emotional stability in the men with whom we have relationships**.

25. Avoid people who want to suck you into their misery. Neither person grows or changes.

On Your Own

I ask, "*What do you want from me?*"
    How can I breathe life for you
        Without my lungs bursting?
You want to lose your very self within me-
    To suck the very breath out of me.
Why give me the total responsibility?
Take back your life and breathe on your own.
    Your energy must come from the universe,
And from people who have become one with it.

26. **When we avoid being hurt in relationships by closing off ourselves, our isolation causes greater hurts. Then we lose the meaning of love – the ability to give love.**

27. Parents give their children permission to mistreat them because they don't feel worthy of more.

28. If you are going to be angry, at least direct it at the right person or thing.

29. Don't expect your friends to do all the work in the friendship. Call, plan activities, meet their needs too.

30. If you get pregnant to hold on to a man, you destroy three lives.

31. Receive other people's love and quit fearing they will take it away.

32. It's a whole lot easier to say what you think you should say than what you feel, but the price in the long run is a whole lot higher.

33. The perfect sister is one whom you can tell your deepest, darkest secret because she won't tell anyone – mainly because she's related to you and doesn't want anyone to know how bad you are!

34. Sisters also understand how nutty your mother is because she was there.

Looking Within

I was afraid to let you see my face without makeup,
But I couldn't keep clogging my pores
Just to have a pretty face.
So my *natural beauty*
Became a cloudy blur down the drain
And out came my imperfect face.
You didn't scream
And no disappointment showed on your face.
And then I realized
That you had always been looking within
And not just at the drugstore base.

Steps to Success

Everyone said they envied us-
    Our wild and active pace.
Little did they know, we used it,
    To cover up our empty lives, we couldn't face.
Being home alone would make us have to deal
    With problems *we'd rather not feel*.

1. Procrastination is as lethal than failure.

2. When you have to do something you hate, pretend you are an actress playing a part.

3. Life has to have balance: spiritual, mental and physical. If you neglect any of these, you will fall down.

4. *Your brain works like a computer. Both can input and output one thing at a time. Worries and stress keep you from being able to think productively.*

5. *Stay alive,*
   Feel fully alive,
   Express that aliveness.

6. Let nothing or no one steal your time.

7. Instead of taking chances on lotteries and contests, take a chance on yourself. The odds are 1:1.

8. At times you do have to follow your gut instincts over the *paralysis of your analysis*.

9. Too much perfection can stifle success.

10. No decision is worse than a wrong decision because you get in the habit of inactivity.

11. Find an abandoned bird's nest and observe the intricate work done instinctively. God has given us instinctive abilities to know what we ought to do, and to become what we ought to be.

12. We can all list our excuses about failure until people who could have really used these excuses became really successful.

13. Promote yourself in business by offering solutions – not problems.

14. Fish will only grow to the size that will accommodate their aquarium. Given a larger space, they will grow larger. We have the power to let our lives grow larger and more significant. Grow by reading, learning, applying and experiencing.

15. We tend to be mirrors reflecting our world instead of true pictures of what we can be.

16. Overcome the fear of being successful.

17. **Initiators are successful people.**

18. Reaching your goal will be empty if you didn't enjoy doing what it took to get there.

19. Those who straddle two rocks worry about falling in and are never safe. If you choose to fulfill your purpose you must devote all of yourself.

He was proud of the success of his life,

And had the stress to prove it.

Until you came along and had toxic stress

Which seemed to out do him.

20. Take care of your stresses or they will overtake you.

21. **Take responsibility and quit asking permission.**

22. The one that never makes a mistake never does anything.

23. The smart way is not to be confused with the easy way.

24. Quit avoiding challenges.

25. Successful women help other women.

26. Ask for letters of recommendation.

27. Creative, inspired, self-fulfilled people are not retired because they are already doing what they want. Join them. Ask, ***"What would I do even if I didn't get paid"*** to find the perfect job for yourself.

28. Every time you take a positive action, you will reinforce your dream of yourself.

29. We get out in troubled water hoping someone will throw a life preserver, instead of preparing and wearing our own safety vest.

30. Spend more time in books than malls.

31. Write down and apply the question, "*What would I do if I knew I could not fail?*" to spiritual, physical, financial and social challenges.

32. BURNOUT: physical, emotional and mental exhaustion. How LONG WOULD IT TAKE YOU TO DECIDE TO GET OFF THE TITANIC! That's how long you should take to decide to change.

33. My greatest heroes are those people who appear to have handicapped lives because they have overcome real challenges in their lives and learned to concentrate on becoming all that they could. On they other hand, **we** who appear to have no handicaps, **live unchallenged lives because of the handicaps we add to our lives.**

34. The acquisition of money is not limited to the chosen few. Your success is not stolen out of my pocket.

35. We all have individual scales to measure our success.

36. **If you're not "getting the picture," it's because you're not focused.**

37. It's a wonderful system – NO ONE REMEMBERS PEOPLE WHO FAIL – *unless they are related to you and they thought you would anyhow*. So what do you have to lose?

38. Your body is a reflection of how you feel about your world.

39. The same "they" who said:
Man can't run a four minute mile,
America will never elect a Catholic President,
You can't invent a light bulb, a car, a radio etc.
etc.,
will tell you that you can't achieve your
purpose in life, and **you can choose to be
forgotten or achieve your own goal of
greatness.**

40. **Seek authority.**

41. We all have individual scales to measure our successes.

42. Model victorious rather than notorious people.

43. ***Goals start with imagination***.

44. Take your job seriously if you are married or single. You won't expect much pay if you work only for extras.

45. You will only get the hard reality when you jump on the easy answer.

*Discovering your
Inner Self*

THE CHILD WITHIN

The child within comes to the door
        And asks if I can come out and play.
But the illusion of Who I Am replies,
            "What will people say?"
    I find it easier and safer
        To be isolated in this person I've created.
All my energy has made
        The multiple persons within
And to strip away the facade
        Would leave the core of me.

Why am I so afraid to let either of us see the real me?
Am I so afraid of feeling vulnerable and free,
When the truth is shown,
Is there any other way to be.
The deception is really more painful
Than the pain.
So we become wounded twice
Because we choose
Not to deal with the
Reality of our lives.

1. A life spent trying to satisfy wants will always be unfulfilled.

2. *The expected rarely gives the solution, the freedom, or the strength.*

3. You can choose to be a stream of life or just a boat floating down the course.

4. Seeking familiarity rather than exploration limits our lives.

5. To feel love in our lives, we must first want it.

6. You must conceive a need to fulfill it.

7. We do everything we can to avoid being with ourselves, *thus killing every hope of happiness.*

8. Be more concerned about *perceiving* yourself than transforming yourself, which will follow anyhow.

9. Seeking approval from others is selling your integrity.

10. Solutions are never found by *ignoring* and *storing* problems.

11. Stop pretending your life is a movie directed by others while you follow a script that keeps your real self hidden.

12. **When you choose to feel victimized,
you forfeit the feeling of being alive**.

13. Leave room for newness in your future.

14. Make your life's decisions on *fulfilling needs* rather than **fear**.

15. Fears may arise after you make an intuitive decision, but you can overcome them.

16. Limitless living assures limitless success.

17. It is a blessing that all your desires in life will never be met.

18. False ideas about what we need to be happy and our true selves cause our unhappiness.

19. *THANK GOD, MOST OF US AREN'T WHO WE THINK WE ARE!*

20. You can't reject a part of you or what happened to you and accept yourself totally.

21. Hiding the truth about ourselves is like trying to cover yourself with a blanket that is too small – *something is always peeking out*.

22. Opening yourself versus fighting with life offers peace and happiness.

23. What's going on inside you affects you more than everything going on in the world.

24. Acknowledge that our empty feeling within comes from unwillingness to look within for our true feelings.

Boy did I have a rotten time!
  She kept talking about how she'd never be perfect,
    How they'd never like her
        If they found out who she really was.
        What if she didn't like herself any better
                Than she thought they did.

And then I looked in the mirror
    And started on my venture to discover.
          And I saw that the truth of who I am
          Is all that there will ever be.

What if I call on my strengths
And they fail me?
What will hold me up?
But isn't that why they call them strengths-
Because they never fail,
We only fail to use them.
It's hard to look in the mirror
And see those sad eyes
For they reveal the truth about our lives.
They reflect the pain
We've had to endure
When we try to coneal
The truth about our feelings.

25. You will see the *angels* inhabiting the earth if you **open your inner mind to them**.

26. You have a built-in answering machine that is taking messages from people who come to inform you, if you replay their words and act.

27. Use time saving devices to free yourself for more time to spend within yourself.

28. Takers lose the rewards of giving.

29. What is true is true. You don't have to defend truth.

30. **Fear is powerless unless you help it.**

31. Become aware when your body tells you exactly what it needs ***nutritionally, emotionally and physically.***

32. You will never really know yourself because God has given us such depths and abilities. The journey to uncovering is the most exciting trip you will ever take.

To M. C. Watts

I must love this miserable state I'm in,
Because I've chosen to stay there
Since a quarter past ten.
I know my mind can only think of one thing at a time
So I keep focusing on making misery mine.
But what if I choose to find a better space,
Could imagination find peace
in a private place?

33. *A mid-life crisis is not inevitable for those who have mended their childhood hurts*. Defense mechanisms built as a child needs to be replaced with strengths.

34. Kites and balloons always fascinate us. They appear to have freedom, but the kite is always tied to the ground and dependent on the wind. The balloon is free to go, but at the whim of the winds. The wind should be what fascinates us because of its power, threats and forming ability. *Be a power like the wind* .

35. Have goals for your inner and outer needs.

36. When you feel really alive, you don't question the meaning of life.

37. ***It is really impossible to be alone***. You may feel alone in a crowd or by yourself, but loneliness can be overcome with the realization that the best person you should know is inside you.

   Inwardly and outwardly, it is better to be alone than to keep bad company.

   Guy Finley

38. If the same problems keep appearing, you haven't found the real answer.

39. A real problem exists behind the apparent problem to which you must seek a solution.

40. *Feeling alive comes from within.*

41. *Reveal and then deal with your most shameful secret.*

42. Your future is not going to be any happier than it is today if you don't make any changes.

43. You don't have to be hard on the outside to have strength of character and determined will.

44. Baby elephants are tied to a stake they can't pull up. Adult elephants could easily pull up the stake, but they don't because they think they can't. **WHAT ELEPHANT THINKING IS LIMITING YOUR SUCCESS?**

45. *Learn to play again.*

46. All improvement in life begins with improvement in our mental pictures.

47. Typewriters signal when you make a mistake or get to close to the edge. **Our signal is our conscience. Listen to it.**

48. **Develop power through decisiveness.**

49. If you haven't found where you are creative, you can't stop looking.

50. *We wrongly consider God our last resort after we've tried everyone else.*

51. Think of the amount of courage you would have if something were attacking your children. Then you'll know how much courage is within you to face your fears and know the Truth.

52. Turn up the volume of your inner voice.

53. *Your main concern should be how you feel.*

54. We wait for the reviews to come in as if our lives were plays trying to please an audience. When in reality, we are the only valid reviewer.

55. If you are not happy with the circle of your life, look within yourself to discover what you need, and then you will know what to do to find the fulfillment you want.

56. The ball and chain thinking we do about past mistakes and other people's expectations or lack of expectations, is only broken by the revelations of our sub-conscious mind.

57. *Others will handicap you with their inadequacies, fears, limited thinking, and jealousness*. When it comes time to account for your life, you will stand alone and take full responsibility. *So why not take responsibility now while you can make changes?*

58. **GET REAL.**

59. Seek divine inspiration and have a good
    attitude to achieve superior results.

60. God has prepared safe havens for us.
    Our bodies go into shock when the pain is
    too great, our minds can focus on peace
    and happiness, and our spirit can call on
    His Spirit.

Checked my DNA?

Lord, are you sure you haven't made a mistake?
　　Maybe confused me with another namesake?
While my fears keep tearing me down,
　You keep building me up to make me complete again.

Lord, are you sure you haven't made a mistake?
　　Have you thought about checking my DNA?
　Yes, my ignorance does make me fearful,
　　But You have already empowered me,
　　　Led me to my purpose and opened up the way.

Self Acceptance

Who is this person trying to be alone with me!
Can't you see that I prefer to watch TV!
If I spend time alone with me,
I fear that I'll see what's really wrong,
But on the other hand,
Maybe I'll see
All the things that are right with me.
Self acceptance is probably the key
For me to be happy being me.

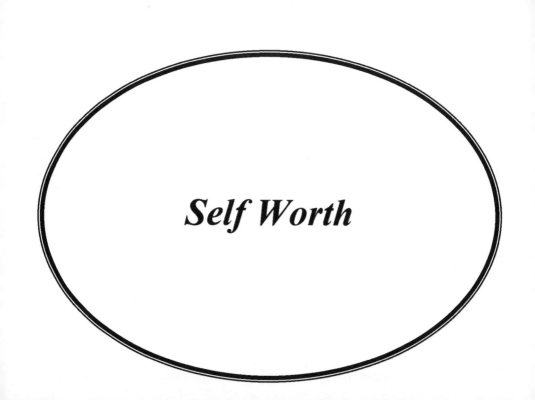

Self Worth

Self Worth

I've quit worrying whether
    You think that I'm somebody

Because I Know
    The Somebody That I Am.

1. You better know who you are or others will define you.

2. Your original you is better than any imitation of whom you try to be.

3. Women will achieve better treatment when women put more value on being a woman.

4. **No one has authority over you unless you have given them permission.**

5. You are only poor if you think you are. Many people, who grew up surrounded by love, carried that wealth, and it grew because they spread it around.

6. Some wives, like Sisyphus in mythology, who had to push a stone uphill only to have it roll back the moment he thought he reached the top, try to push their husbands. They should use their energy to push themselves to the top.

7. Quit measuring yourself by male standards.

8. **Women with high self esteem don't have one night stands.**

9. Secure self-worth remains the same regardless of praise or criticism.

10. **If we worked as hard at developing self-worth in our children as clothing them in designer clothes, there would be a new generation of happy adults.**

11. The amount of money you make has nothing to do with your self-worth.

12. **You already have everything within you to be complete** – you need to use what you have been given.

13. If you delude yourself with fantasies, when the true appraisal comes, like on a zirconium ring, your life will be deemed worthless.

14. People who feel inferior have the need to put you down.

15. *Validate yourself and you won't need it from others.*

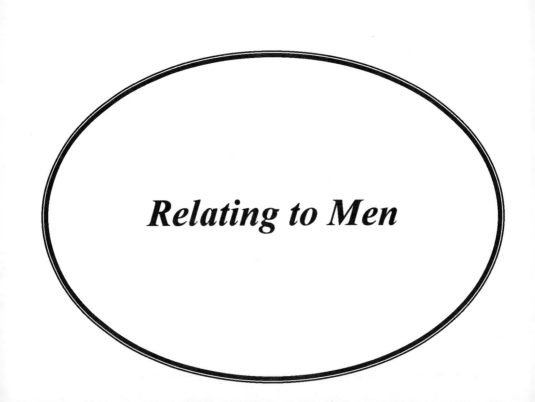

Relating to Men

1. Wonder why men's magazines don't have articles like:
   How Can You Get Her to Marry You
   How Can You Sexually Please Your Woman
   How Can You Keep your Wife Faithful.

2. We've heard enough and endured enough macho men.

3. Remember, men start the wars, and the women are raped by the invader to get back at the men.

4. Call (202) 307-3126, the Bureau of Prisons, to find out if a man has ever been in prison.

5. Seek men who are vulnerable and can show their feelings.

6. Some wives, like Sisyphus in mythology, who had to push a stone uphill only to have it roll back the moment he thought he reached the top, try to push their husbands. They should use their energy to push themselves to the top.

7.   Quit measuring yourself by male standards.

8.   **Women with high self esteem don't have one night stands.**

9.   Your self-worth should remain the same regardless of whether a man praises or criticizes you.

10. Men believe in recycling — *when they find a new wife, they expect you to give her your stationery*.

11. **A controlling man will only see you at certain times.**

12. Find a man who reads books about the differences between men and women and seeks to understand you better.

13. Men think that every woman they meet wants to marry them.

14. If you're not a man's Saturday night date and he says:

   My ex in-laws are visiting me,

   My boss makes me work on Saturday nights,

   I do my laundry or grocery shopping on Saturday nights,

   —You are not important in his life.

15. You have the right to check your mate's faithfulness because he may infect you.

16. Men get angry about something else when they know you are going to be angry about what they haven't done.

17. You can keep eating the crumbs of a relationship if you want to feel like a

BUG.

18. Recreational sex will leave you as empty as recreational mud fighting – you don't know the person any better and you have the feeling of mud all over you.

19. **Send a single rose to a man you admire**. You don't have to sign your name, since the pleasure will come from the doing rather than the thank you.

20. Women take chances on the men in their lives rather than themselves.

21. Shallow men only aroused by sexual trappings are playing a game where you will always lose. *Sexual satisfaction* – love, care, intimacy – *is not achieved by wearing sexy lingerie anymore than putting on a bathing suit makes you an Olympic swimmer.*

22. Men claim that it's all right to go to a nude bar, but they clear out when a video camera is turned on them.

23. **Timing in relationships makes a big difference**. It's like trying to sweeten tea that has gotten cold; it never tastes the same.

24. *You may love a man with all your heart, but please keep your brain!*

25. It is as important to hear what he is not saying as what he is saying.

26. If there are 82,000 men and 5,000 women in prison for murder, who do you think you need to be more careful about?

27. Men, like presents, are sometimes wrapped very expensively to disguise that there isn't much to the gift.

28. Women involved in quick-sand relationships will be swallowed by the muck pulling them down.

To love you might be too hard
Or cause me pain.
I think I can't bear the pain,
So I'll barely try,
And then when love fails
It won't hurt much
Because I didn't give much, anyhow.

The Call

He didn't call tonight-
　　First you told yourself
　　　　You wouldn't let it bother you,
　　It didn't mean a thing.
　　　　　But as the time passed
　　　　　　　The more angry you became.
　　　　　Wouldn't it have been easier
　　　　　　　Not to have someone to wait on to call?
　　　　You didn't want to lose your control
　　　　　　　And risk feeling sadness.

But what made you sleep
　　　Just fine that night was
　　　　　　You were honest enough to admit
　　That you did care if he called,
　　And you wished he had,
　　　　　　But if he didn't,
　You chose to think no less of yourself or him.

Your place or my place
　　　She said in her most liberated way.
　　Why not try this aerobic exercise,
　　　　In the bed by 10, out by 11:05!
For centuries men have been having sex
With a *No Name* and *Pretty Face.*
　　What's this empty feeling
That's come in this heart of mine?
I thought it would be so much fun
　　To use him like some cheap wine.
　　But when I glanced in the mirror
　　　I had again become
Miss *No Name* with a *Pretty Face.*

Success after Divorce

Divorce demands and requires changes. You can try to resist those changes and become a victim, or you can take control of your life through inner thinking. Quit relying on your old, rut thinking or reactionary thinking based on fear, anxiety, self-doubt and negativity.

Whether you are now married, newly divorced or a seasoned veteran, I think you can learn from the following instructions. After a divorce, friends think they help by offering sympathy. The friends that you need are those who support the truth - **that you will survive, you are open to new opportunities and directions,** *and you must become strong!* You need friends who say "*You can do it*," and to yourself you need to say, "**I have the strength and power within for self awakening and happiness.**"

Divorces evoke a lot of self-pity and poor me thinking. Of course, at the time, you are experiencing extreme stress, but you don't have to live with it any longer than you choose. *The role of victim is self-defeating and degrading.* Yes, no matter what has happened to you, you get the opportunity to start over.

You have lost the crutch of blaming your mate for your failures to take action, find happiness, and to attain your wants. **You gain the responsibility for individualized intuitive, creative, and power thinking**. One of the worse errors in thinking is that our mate is keeping us from becoming what we think we want to be. *What a crock!*

You can control your thinking, your reactions, and your beliefs about yourself. Marriage vows say love and honor; they don't say give away your thinking abilities, self-worth, or individualism. Marriage does not give one spouse the added responsibility or control of the other spouse's becoming whom they need to be. And because you have given over your thinking decisions to someone else does not mean that you can't take back your life.

Your mate is no longer the person you married. The divorcing spouse is going to put his/her needs first. **Take care of yourself. Learn to make your own decisions**. The truth for all situations will come from within.

You can choose not to feel unhappy about your divorce. You don't want unhappiness. Be honest about the condition of your marriage. It was not working for either of you even if only one spouse chooses to make a change.

Replacing a relationship without inner changes will result in the same problem relationship. Negative attitudes, reflected in fault finding, self pity, and escape prevent productive growth.

Release blame. *You can not change the past*. Focus on the present moment and be single-minded toward becoming the person you are meant to be.

Quit focusing on feeling deprived. Yes, you have taken great losses on financial security, lifestyle and trust, but you are not a lost person. These things are not you. The greater loses are self-esteem, self-confidence, approval, and identity. Resolve to reestablish your true self. If you find that you gave away yourself in marriage, take yourself back!

Grow by expanding and encouraging your own thinking. Never say I, "I have given him to best years of my life." You have to power to choose to make the rest of your life what you want it to be. **Flourish!** Begin to WONDER.

The newness of now has no opposites and therefore knows no opposition. That is why your sincere wish to start over cannot help but succeed.

Guy Finley THE SECRET WAY OF WONDER

Drop the false expectations of what you thought your life would be, so that you can discover the wonderful process of unfolding what life really has to offer.

Instead of concentrating your efforts on trying to find a new mate, learn to know yourself with searching and unfolding within. Like a wounded doe, the newly divorced ventures into the dating world and goes through a succession of males who are either professional singles, alcoholic, co-dependent, emotionally dead or financially bankrupt. Before she has figures out what went wrong with the last marriage, she becomes involved with a whole new set of problems. The divorced seek validation through a new mate.

Some specific steps to follow before dating:

- Read, read, and read more on self-esteem, self-worth, healing emotions and inner power and goals.
- Learn to cherish solitude as a time needed to reflect, mediate, and let your inner self be revealed to you. These are not group activities.
- Reestablish a relationship with yourself:
- Create a vision from within rather than the one others have placed on you. After any divorce, there is a period of depression, but you must get active and revitalize your energy. **Renew your faith in yourself. Praise yourself for what you've done right. Say only good things to yourself.**

The moment you become unemotionally involved with your ex is when your feeling about divorce will change for the better. Then you can focus on the present moment and begin to feel ALIVE. Concentrate on your children's needs. You do not need to seek a replacement for their father. The emotional highs and lows of dating a man who has not gone through his own healing process will add additional havoc to your life.

Ask your friends for the names of women who have been divorced for several years and talk to them with the following stipulations. Don't ask them to listen to the details of your divorce. It serves no useful purpose because you are there to learn from them.

Determine whether they have dropped their past baggage and are in a continual inner growth process. Get away from women with negative outlooks.

Remember, you are not looking for someone to do your thinking, you are seeking to learn from their mistake and successes.. The mentor must be willing to reveal themselves to you.

Personal growth will not start where revenge and hatred are festering. These two malices will keep you physically and emotionally ill. Rebelling against your personal values and beliefs will not give you relief or answers.

Divorce is a trauma equal to the death of a spouse. Unlike that situation, there isn't a funeral, and the process is strung out because you still probably have to be involved with your ex if there's children. None of us married and planned for it to end in divorce. Either the partners were incapable or there was no growth toward the common goal of completeness. Did you stop and ask *"What were we working toward, anyhow?"* If you are totally honest, your expectations were not being met. *Aren't you tired of settling for less than you deserve?*

Re-exam the truth about your thinking processes. Wives, unfortunately, tend to turn over their thinking to their husbands. Take back the decision making - you will be forced to anyhow. You have a built in **"life instinct"** that works toward success, don't thwart it. Remember when you were your strongest. **You can be that person again, even stronger.**

Emotions and feelings are continually stuffed, or ignored in unhappy marriages. It takes some work to channel them into productive outlays. After all, **you can only heal what you feel**. Disassociating and denial become inappropriate avenues. You must be willing to feel life's sadness to feel life's happiness.

When you do start to date, the single best advice is to ask, "*How does this person make me feel?*" Do some in depth thinking and writing about the kind of person you want. Are you developed enough to be the person they will want?

Good committed relationships heal our past wounds.

Order Form

Want additional copies of this book? Life's Instruction Book for Women, and Life's Instruction Book for Women , Volume II make great gifts for friends.

Each book is $ 5.95. Please add $2.00 per book for postage and handling. Georgia residents must include 5% state sales tax. (Canadian order must be accompanied by postal money order in U.S. funds.) Allow two weeks for delivery. Send check payable to:

BARBARA GRAY PROACTIVES
399 Old Canton Road
Marietta, Georgia 30068
(404) 971-0179